WEEKLY WR READER
EARLY LEARNING LIBRARY

HOW SIMPLE MACHINES WORK

# HOW PULLEYS WORK

by **Jim Mezzanotte**

**Reading consultant:  Susan Nations, M.Ed.,**
author/literacy coach/consultant

**Science and curriculum consultant:  Debra Voege, M.A.,**
science and math curriculum resource teacher

Please visit our web site at: www.garethstevens.com
For a free color catalog describing Weekly Reader® Early Learning Library's list
of high-quality books, call 1-877-445-5824 (USA) or 1-800-387-3178 (Canada).
Weekly Reader® Early Learning Library's fax: (414) 336-0164.

Library of Congress Cataloging-in-Publication Data

Mezzanotte, Jim.
    How pulleys work / by Jim Mezzanotte.
        p. cm. — (How simple machines work)
    Includes bibliographical references and index.
    ISBN-10: 0-8368-7348-3 — ISBN-13: 978-0-8368-7348-1 (lib. bdg.)
    ISBN-10: 0-8368-7353-X — ISBN-13: 978-0-8368-7353-5 (softcover)
    1. Pulleys—Juvenile literature. I. Title.
    II. Series: Mezzanotte, Jim. How simple machines work.
    TJ1103.M49    2006
    621.8—dc22                                        2006008667

This edition first published in 2007 by
**Weekly Reader® Early Learning Library**
A Member of the WRC Media Family of Companies
330 West Olive Street, Suite 100
Milwaukee, WI  53212  USA

Copyright © 2007 by Weekly Reader® Early Learning Library

Managing editor: Mark J. Sachner
Art direction: Tammy West
Cover design, page layout, and illustrations: Dave Kowalski
Photo research: Sabrina Crewe

Picture credits: cover, title © Susan Van Etten/PhotoEdit; p. 5 © Neil Rabinowitz/CORBIS;
p. 8: © James P. Blair/CORBIS; p. 9 © Mary Kate Denny/PhotoEdit; p. 10 © Alison
Wright/CORBIS; pp. 16, 20 © Royalty-Free/CORBIS; p. 18 © Buddy Mays/CORBIS;
p. 21 © Randy Faris/CORBIS

Printed in the United States of America

1 2 3 4 5 6 7 8 9 10 09 08 07 06

# TABLE OF CONTENTS

**Cover and title page:** The cranes in this picture use many pulleys at once to lift huge containers onto ships.

# CHAPTER

## THE WORLD OF PULLEYS

Have you ever ridden a bike or raised a flag up a flagpole? If so, then you have used a pulley. Pulleys make it easier to move things. They help people in many ways.

Pulleys can be found in all kinds of places. People use them in their homes to raise window blinds. On a sailboat, sailors use them to **hoist** sails. Many engines have pulleys. Big cranes use pulleys to lift heavy loads. Tow trucks have pulleys, and so do escalators. Pulleys are all around you!

On sailboats, people use pulleys to lift heavy sails.

# CHAPTER

## HOW PULLEYS WORK

You can make your own pulley. Find a closet where you hang clothes. Then find a bucket with a handle. Tie one end of a rope to the handle. Throw the other end over the closet bar. Now, pull down on that end. The bucket goes up. You now have a pulley.

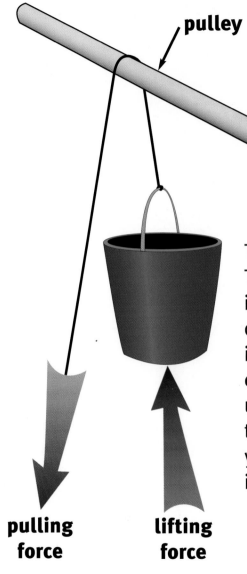

**pulley**

**pulling force**

**lifting force**

The closet bar is your pulley. This pulley has helped you in an important way. It has changed your pulling **force** into a lifting force. You pull down, but the bucket goes up. Pulling down is easier than lifting up. You can use your weight to help. **Gravity** is on your side!

grooved wheel

rope

These children are using pulleys. The ropes move in grooved wheels.

A pulley is usually a wheel with a groove in it. The rope fits in the groove. A grooved wheel works better than a closet bar. It cuts down on **friction**. Friction is anything that keeps things from moving smoothly. The rope moves easily in the turning pulley.

You raise a flag just like you raised the bucket. The flagpole has a pulley on top. A loop of rope hangs from it. The flag is attached to one side of the loop. You pull down on the other side. As you pull down, the flag goes up.

As this man pulls on the rope, the flag will travel upward.

Not all pulleys have ropes. Some have chains or **cables**. A cable is like a metal rope. It is very strong, so it can lift heavy loads.

As a cable moves on pulleys, this cable car goes up the hill. Then it goes back down.

# CHAPTER

## KINDS OF PULLEYS

A flagpole has a **fixed pulley**. The pulley stays in one place, on top of the flagpole. A **moveable pulley** is different. It is attached to the **load** being lifted.

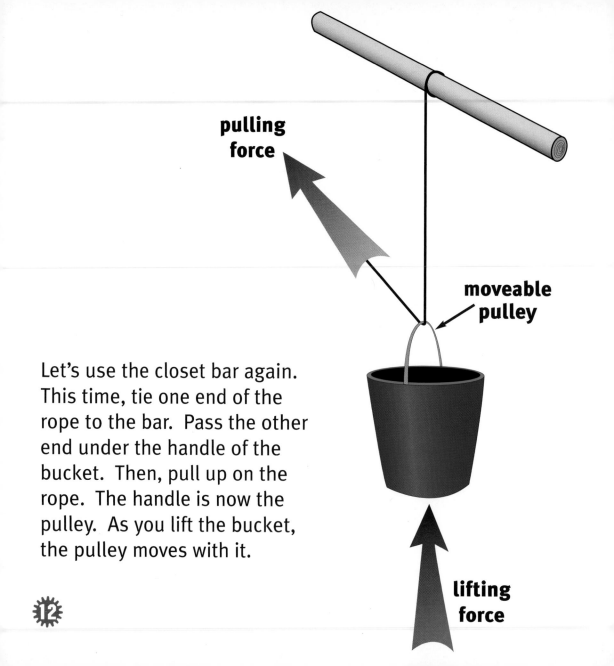

**pulling force**

**moveable pulley**

Let's use the closet bar again. This time, tie one end of the rope to the bar. Pass the other end under the handle of the bucket. Then, pull up on the rope. The handle is now the pulley. As you lift the bucket, the pulley moves with it.

**lifting force**

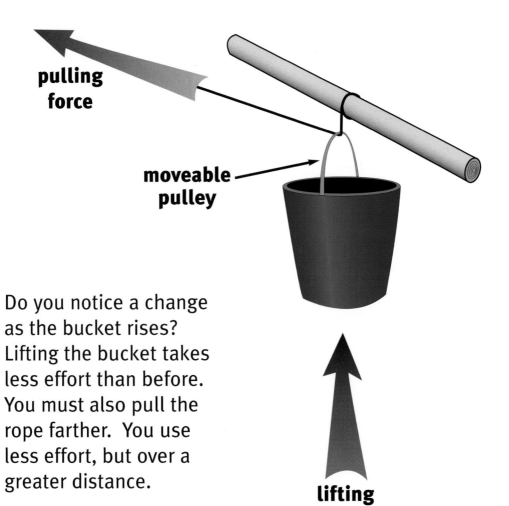

**pulling force**

**moveable pulley**

Do you notice a change as the bucket rises? Lifting the bucket takes less effort than before. You must also pull the rope farther. You use less effort, but over a greater distance.

**lifting force**

13

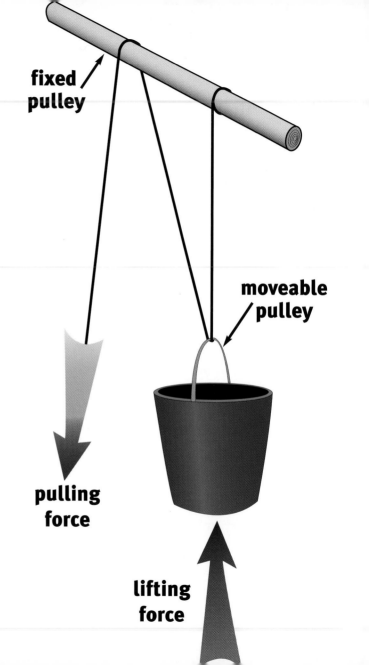

Do you want to make your job even easier? Throw the end of your rope over the bar. You have just added a pulley. The handle is a moveable pulley. The bar is a fixed pulley. Pull down on the rope. Remember, pulling down is easier. This system of pulleys is called **block and tackle**.

**fixed pulley**

**moveable pulley**

**pulling force**

**lifting force**

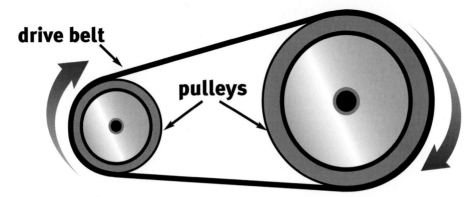

drive belt

pulleys

Some pulleys use a drive belt. The belt is a loop between two pulleys. One pulley turns, or drives, the other pulley. Many cars have drive belts to help their engines. If one pulley is smaller, it turns faster. Both pulleys turn in the same direction.

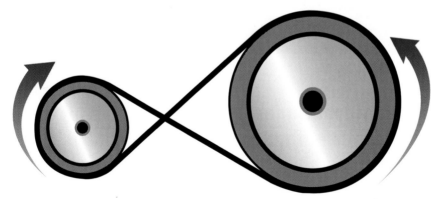

If the belt is crossed, however, the second pulley turns in the opposite direction.

Rock climbers use a rope and pulley to use less effort to lower themselves down steep rock faces.

Pulleys are **simple machines**. They let you do a lot of work without a lot of effort. In this case, "work" just means moving something. Today, a lot of machines are complicated. But they are often many simple machines working together.

# CHAPTER  4

## JOBS FOR PULLEYS

Pulleys have been around for a long time. One early pulley might have been a rope thrown over a tree branch so a worker could lower a basket of apples to the ground. Today, machines use pulleys for many jobs.

A crane lifts heavy loads with strong cables and pulleys. The cables hang down from a long arm, called the **jib**. The cables have a hook or a claw on the end for lifting things.

jib

cables

pulleys

claw

You can see the big pulleys on this crane.

The cranes in this picture use many pulleys
at once to lift huge containers onto ships.

Often cranes use many pulleys at once to lift their loads.
You may see these pulleys wherever ships or trains are
being loaded with heavy equipment.

A bike chain works like a drive belt. A wheel with teeth turns the chain at the front of the bike. The chain drives the rear wheel.

Many machines use drive belts. Engines use drive belts for turning different parts. Sewing machines and washing machines use them, too. A bike chain is a kind of drive belt. When you pedal, the chain drives the rear wheel.

Ski lifts and elevators use pulleys. Big **oil derricks** do, too. Sailboats have many pulleys. Using pulleys, one sailor can hoist a big sail. When you need to move something, a pulley will usually help!

Ski lifts use cables and pulleys to move skiers up a hill.

# GLOSSARY

**cables:** strong metal lines made from strands of thick wire

**block and tackle:** a system of moveable and fixed pulleys that makes it easy to lift heavy objects

**fixed pulley:** a pulley that stays attached to a point above the load

**force:** the strength or energy used to cause something to move or change

**friction:** anything that keeps two surfaces from moving against each other easily

**gravity:** the force that pulls everything toward the center of Earth. Your weight is really the pulling force of gravity.

**hoist:** raise something, such as a flag or sail, by using ropes and pulleys

**jib:** the long arm on a crane

**load:** anything that a pulley system is lifting or otherwise pulling

**moveable pulley:** a pulley that moves with the load as the load is lifted

**oil derricks:** large towers that hold the machinery used to drill for oil

**simple machines:** devices with few or no moving parts. They let you do a lot of work without a lot of effort.

# FOR MORE INFORMATION

## BOOKS

*Pulleys.* Early Bird Physics (series). Sally M. Walker and Roseann Feldmann (Lerner Publications)

*Pulleys and Gears.* Machines in Action (series). Angela Royston (Heinemann)

*Sensational Science Projects with Simple Machines.* Fantastic Physical Science Experiments (series). Robert Gardner (Enslow Publishers)

## WEB SITES

### Edheads: Simple Machines
*edheads.org/activities/simple-machines/*
At this interactive site, you can learn all about simple machines, including pulleys.

### Mikids.com: Simple Machines
*www.mikids.com/Smachines.htm*
This site has examples of simple machines, including pulleys. It also has fun activities to help you learn more about simple machines.

# INDEX

## About the Author

**Jim Mezzanotte** has written many books for children. He lives in Milwaukee with his wife and two sons. He uses simple machines every day.